SMALL TALK SYMPHONY

poems by

Joshua Lillie

Finishing Line Press
Georgetown, Kentucky

SMALL TALK SYMPHONY

ACKNOWLEDGMENTS

Thank you to all my English and art teachers for encouraging teenage me to
keep going.

I'd be nowhere without the opportunities given to me by Write Bloody
Publishing, *Stanchion Zine, Black Lily Zine, Wildscape Literary Journal,
Universes Poetry Journal, Sonora Review, Tarry Lit,* Unleash Press, and
Finishing Line Press. Thank you for helping get my work out into the world.

Immense gratitude to all who've supported me by reading the various,
endlessly-changing drafts of my poems.

Publisher: Leah Huete de Maines
Editor: Christen Kincaid
Cover Art: Madeleine Allenegui
Author Photo: Will Austin Photography
Cover Design: Elizabeth Maines McCleavy

Order online: www.finishinglinepress.com
also available on amazon.com

Author inquiries and mail orders:
Finishing Line Press
PO Box 1626
Georgetown, Kentucky 40324
USA

Contents

YOU BUILD A HOUSE

You build a house and eventually,
you won't need the tools anymore.

For years, they take up space
in every available drawer.

The hammers stay accessible and the shovels
stay out, leaned against all the half-painted walls.

The pickax stays sharp and the wheelbarrow
unburdened by cobwebs.

The hope is that one day, there will be a place
for everything and everything will be in its place.

Everything will be affixed in its proper position,
and you can return the measuring tape

to the toolbox, and the hammers
and the screwdrivers and the stud-finder too.

This is what the analysts tell you,
that the horizon is reachable

but it is miles away. Years and years away.
One day the tools will be a reflex in your limbs,

your fingertips of sharpened lead will tighten
the loose doorknobs on their own. One day

you can move mountains of dirt with trial and error
alone. You can patch the deep holes

with the whole heart of experience. The teachers
can only teach you what to forget, who to forgive.

You've got to learn to build memories
and to build trust in new futures all on your own.

YOU'RE PAINTING A FENCE

The fence will take twelve years
to finish painting. For twelve years
people will pass you painting and tell you
they could finish that fence anytime
they wanted. From the window, your father
will yell down that he's been painting fences
since he was a boy and he could paint fences
around you. But none of these people see
all the decades of old paint layered beneath
the fresh coats, or all the little cracks
in the wood that soak up half of each day,
or all the rounded corners that inherited
their angles from colder, harsher winters.
These people never realize that their fence
is a prison that will harden and fade.
They see the sky and clouds and the grass
growing high but never separate the blue sky
from the prison bars painted sky blue.

HOLY TOMORROW

Nobody even notices the antique chandelier
up in the eaves until nightfall, when someone
lights the candles. When someone flips a switch.

Nobody talks about how we have chandeliers
to thank for disco balls, how we have the town fool
to thank for neon signs. Nobody notices that there's only

one sandwich left until there are zero sandwiches left.
If done expertly, the playlist will transition from song to song
without anybody noticing that they've been up and dancing

all night long. If left to an algorithm, the radio might jump
from new-wave to honky-tonk without warning and you'll
be caught with your arms flailing in contradictory statements.

If you're the song everybody dances to, then I'm the song
that leaves them nostalgic for the good old days, the song
that leaves them wanting more when there's nothing left.

ANYWHERE EXTRA-STRENGTH

After I first heard that everyone puts their pants on
one leg at a time, I started tossing my jeans onto the ground,
jumping into the holes and pulling them up both legs at once,
in a single motion.

I used to lie that slicing onion didn't water my eyes and for years
I had to hold back tears at barbecues. After the hundredth person
told me I looked like I needed a cheeseburger, I started filling
my pockets with lettuce leaves, in case I found myself in a pinch.

To tell someone they looked like they *didn't* need a cheeseburger
is something that's only recently occurred to me, after the one
hundred and first person saw me eating my first carrot of the day
and told me they'd never seen a domesticated rabbit uncaged.

I TRY TO BE A DOG

I get on all fours and bark and beg and lick
my balls but no one believes me at my age.
I've been practicing my growl since
second grade, when the neighbor's big dogs
started to sniff around at night for
the neighborhood cat. When you're a kid
you decide one day you're the family cat,
and your parents go along with it. You meow
and purr and chase after rainbows
in the window and you really, truly believe
that your parents believe that you're a cat.
You never hear them ask *what happened*
to our son? Has our son been kidnapped? Should we
alert the authorities? and you never wonder
why they're not more concerned.
They continue their chores and they stop
to pet you and feed you treats and watch you
pretend to sleep on the arm of the couch
and this is enough. You're a housecat now.
That's all you'll need to be for years to come.

SCHRÖDINGER'S CARAFE

A question mark in a poem is like a cherry
on top of a cherry. We're not getting to
the bottom of anything! An exclamation point

in an opening line is like a grand-opening banner
in the sky. Bottomless mimosas are open-ended
questions, dollar menus wielding infinity
in the lunch-hour of the beholder.

But where does bottomless belong
on the half-full/half-empty spectrum?
At once too much and not enough, it depends
on how dressed to impress you are.

BROKEN HEART SYNDROME

My wife told me a story she heard on NPR,
a scientific account of a husband dying
from a broken heart twenty-three weeks
after his wife died in her sleep.
The story said that the survivors develop
hypertension over the months spent coping
with the stress and heartbreak of loss.
She told me that if she dies to remember
to schedule an appointment to monitor
my heart. She didn't say it, but it hung
in the air that if I died first, she would do
the same.

SIMMERING ALIVE

We're out here chasing dopamine vicariously,
watching the passersby scrape joy

off barstools like twice-chewed gum,
from between snake eyes in the tumbled dice,

watching them chase the trail of dust trailing
off the carrot dangling off the dragon's tail.

Inflatable tube men deter me the way
wooden owls deter sky-worn doves.

I'm following the neon arrows that lead to neon
open signs that lead to neon construction zones

that light the detour home. Buy the ticket, take
the ride, but this parking spot is reserved

and I can't afford to miss this appointment.
They can't pigeon-spike the park benches

because the city can't distinguish a wallet
from an empty pocket. But they also can't charge

a taxpayer twice for the same empty seat.
Some department stores have equipped their walls

with loudspeakers enshrined in barbwire that funnel
out classical muzak at an unbearably high volume,

in an attempt to weaken loiterers at their doors. So
I've started stockpiling secondhand trombones and

violins and parking them in vacant handicap spots,
free to anyone who wants to play.

SENSE OF DIRECTION

From the plane the docks look like safety
pins, keeping the mainland from floating
through the bay. The commuter bridge
from so high divides the water like clenched teeth
in a zipper fly. The outlet store is shaped like
a typewriter and the landing gear pops out
like toast. From sleep

I awake in the fetal position, no matter
how flat out and straight I dozed off. In yoga
I return to child's pose most comfortably,
reluctant to leave the womb.

I've never had to know just where I am
or where I'm going. I've had mothers, wives
and iPhone navigation. I'll never hide as well
as killdeers in the shrubs. On the beaten path,
I'm swallowing bugs. I'm bushwhacking frogs.
My sense of direction leaves entire continents
to be desired.

MODERN CAMOUFLAGE

I fold all my clothes into luggage
with no getaway plans: good to go,
nowhere to be.

In case of fire, I keep my valuables
in disaster-proof safes. My proof
of insurance is a laminated shipwreck.

My shoes have hidden compartments
beneath the insoles, where it's convenient
to hide gunpowder, but these days
that's where I keep hydroxyzine,
anti-inflammatories and allergy spray.

In case of flood,
this pistachio shell doubles as a flotation
device. In case of gas leak,
this wallpaper mimics a forest in peacetime,
where even the canopies could be outposts
armed in disguise.

A LOT OF MONEY

My stepdad used to brag that
he always had at least a hundred dollars
in his wallet, everywhere he went.
And maybe that *was* a lot of money
in two thousand and two, in that
dry county, in that part of town,
in that two-story home that overlooked
that small town's largest trailer park.
My mom divorced him a long time ago,
and tomorrow he'll be two years dead,
but every time I pull out my wallet
I think about how I've always kept
two hundred dollars in there at all times,
just so I can feel that I'm ahead of him
that much more.

BLURRED FACES ON THE EVENING NEWS

Psych ward admissions on the medical history
charts are to artists what nine bullet wounds are
to war heroes, or charred teeth to fire-breathers.
Shot means shot but *shot to death* implies it took
more than a single bullet.

Thirty-five is a lot to pay for a lunch special,
but if it's years we're talking about that's barely
enough time to get lost in the desert
and come out civilized at the forest clearing.

You wait your turn to speak to the reporter,
and later, when you see your face blurred
on the news, you tell the world *I may not
be camera-ready, but I'm sure as hell not dead yet.*

PISSED OFF / PAYING ATTENTION

I don't need a therapist I need a partner
in crime, someone to help me overthrow
the status quos. I don't need to learn
to live and let live. I need someone to wait
around the corner in the getaway car,
someone to hold the bottles steady
while I pour the gasoline and fasten
the rags. Someone to empty the basket
as I refill the guillotine.
I don't need a therapist I need someone
to handcuff myself to. Someone
to push the cop over as I crouch down
behind them. Someone to stir the soup
as I hand out bowls to the shelterless.
Someone to press the lever and run
as I overfill each White House toilet with
powdered wigs. Someone to trip
the fire alarm as I release all the animals
at the county zoo. I don't need someone
to charge me two hundred and fifty dollars
an hour to restore my faith in humanity.
I need two hundred and fifty million people
to stop accepting what they can't change,
and altogether change what they cannot
accept.

DEEPER THAN YOU DIG

Remove the father figure. Turn the mother
into a duck. Replace the older brothers
with action figures and the younger one
with a rifle. Write off the two stepbrothers,
the one with the bone-fused ankle bracelet
and the one who slipped flat off the roof, leaving
behind two young daughters and an emigrated
widow. Tell every teacher

and high school girlfriend not to get too attached
because you'll be leaving town any day now.
On your wedding day in lieu of vows
hold up a frame of the meme that says *why
don't kids play outside anymore?* above a picture
of a crowded interstate. Written below:
the outside they built. Replace the father figure
with an anvil and strap your mother into the lake.

Unfriend your brothers and cousins and uncles
and aunts and update your profile picture with
the one from the family reunion when you were
in middle school, where your face is upside down
and everyone else's is haloed in sharpie.
Some men some women hold and feel protected
by the weight of the world. Me, I flatten first.

DOWNSLOPE

The rain scares all the animals away.
I want to see the animals dripping wet,
taking turns treating the downslope
as a slip-and-slide, sunscreen dolloped
on the tips of their noses.
But the animals retreat at even the fewest
of sprinkles, never connecting the drops
to the heavy, grey clouds. The animals
never know how much is coming next.
I love the rain, but I have a roof over my head
and an app that tells me when it will end.
I know we're not going to get much more
than this.

PREDICTIVE TEXT

There are no stupid questions but
these days there's really no excuse.
All of human history is in our pockets.
So are directions to every Pizza Hut
and Taco Bell location on the face of
the earth. *Is there somewhere around here*

where I can buy some cowboy boots?
Don't ask me. Ask Google.
Math teachers told us *when you grow up,*
you won't have a calculator in your pocket
everywhere you go but I'm sorry to say we do.
I'm sorry to say all the ways that history
repeats itself are laid bare in the fields

where civil war battles occurred,
and all the undetonated landmines
are still out there awaiting travelers.
There are entire websites devoted to
other people's mistakes.
There are history books devoted entirely

to what solitary confinement can do
to the soul. But we visit these websites
to look out simulated windows
and we use these books
to keep scratch-paper equations
weighed down on windy days.

SELF-MEDICATING

They call it self-medicating for depression
but that doesn't transmit the image
of the TV glow dimming the living room,
casting light on the crow's feet, like
a timelapse video of how a liter of vodka
disappears. It doesn't de-romanticize
the sound of the crackling fire,
the single rock cooling the heat
off the fingers in grandpa's antique crystal,
the stale, worn softness
of his soiled midnight-to-morning robe.
The image it brings is one of teaspoons
soaring as airplanes in the air,
of ramequins measured out with vitamins,
of slow-moving lines in the other back corner
of the neighborhood pharmacy.
They call it self-medicating for depression
to avoid implying you might be drinking
yourself to death.

THIS FREEDOM SWALLOWS YOU WHOLE

This freedom of the nap is almost over.
This freedom of headline-only breaking news.

This freedom of mimosas without borders.
This freedom of the well that might run dry.

This freedom of air-conditioned waiting rooms.
This freedom of friction burns in your pocket book.

This freedom of where'd I put my pepper spray?
This freedom of the doctor will see you now.

This freedom of first to the finish line wins.
This freedom of dollars rounded up for charity.

This freedom of cannot connect to server,
of ergonomic guns and background checks.

This freedom that grabs you by the ears
and throws you feet first in the swimming hole.

This freedom that twists your insides into
participation trophies and unglues your badge of pride.

That paints pinstripes on your wedding gown.
That drips orange juice down your sleeve.

This freedom serves breakfast till the eggs dry up.
This freedom is running ten minutes behind.

This freedom relieves you of your duty now.
This freedom thanks you for your service, sir.

This freedom's got a belt loop in it, to carry the baggage
that freedom outweighs. This freedom isn't sharpening

its teeth, it's filing yours down to nubs. This freedom
isn't well-equipped it's well-funded and well-insured.

This freedom stockpiles ammunitions in other countries
and plants legal seeds in magazines.

This freedom smells like turpentine and isolates
your skin cells clean like bleach.

This freedom isn't calling for a headcount
it's taking your measurements and folding your sheets.

This freedom is double-meat and double cheese
between two mouthwatering sesame buns.

This freedom mixes well with antibiotics and alcohol.
This freedom takes a village to uphold.

This freedom descends like a lithium prescription
onto the helipad between your shoulders.

This freedom is a minimum charge of eighteen dollars
on your card. This freedom isn't taking applications

at this time but résumés are always encouraged.
This freedom swallows your everlasting soul.

SUNNY SIDE

Fun is a twentieth century invention,
along with rollercoasters, beach vacations
and disposable income. For thousands of years
all we did was survive, to varying degrees
of success. *Are you happy?* was a question

as inconceivable as *is your refrigerator running?*
to a Victorian housemaid. Sometimes an invention
comes along that makes us sleep deeper.
Sometimes one that licks the grease right off
our elbows. Sometimes one that helps us tolerate
the boredom when the fun won't come.

As kids we all drew smoke rings rising
from the chimneys of our homes and a smile
plastered on the sun above us. As adults
we keep our eyes peeled for signs that say
it's 5 o'clock somewhere and chase after
happy hours that never end.

WASTING AWAY IS ONE WAY TO THINK OF IT

Poets shouldn't drink and they know they shouldn't but
they do. Who was the loving memory for before
it was dedicated to your death? The last round was saluted
to a touchdown pass but this one seems more somber.
There are as many tears dripping down the mouth of the glass
as there are bubbles aerating the orange juice in its body.
Your death used to mean my time was coming and so was
everyone's I loved. But today it means too much has passed
since last year when we clinked our glasses together and split
every appetizer on the menu. I saw your cousin from across
the table and today she looks more like you than the baby-faced
assortment of hereditary traits and follicles and inclinations that
you'd remember. At your funeral, you laid open-faced, and
no matter how hard they tried they couldn't blush the yellow
off your cheeks. You were twenty pounds lighter in death
but you wouldn't know it by the look of you, capsized
and bloated there, sunlit like a bumblebee caught
between the half-cracked blinds and the window sealed shut.

BEDRIDDEN

I am bedridden and you are far away.
We'd get where we're going
and you'd have to treat me like a balloon.
Find something to tie me to
why don't you.
Keep me out of harm's way, safe
from the bird's beak and the falling hail.
I feel the asteroid crinkling at the base
of my skull and I see earthquakes
rippling the dust off my anchored soul
and I hear the driveway kicking stones
and the door handle jingling keys
and you walk in with your arms full
of shed snakeskins. I should've known
you hadn't gone far.

THIS DEATH

You'll carry this death with you,
the one sprawled on the couch brushing
cheese puff dust off its chest and about to call it
a day. The near-death in the pop-tart box,
the around-the-corner death of distant memory
that recalls middle school nights spent up
too late and first periods spent catching shuteye
on one load-bearing elbow. The someday-
eventually death that the holidays always conjure,
the smell of cinnamon and spiced rum that
only disappeared from the bottle when sleigh bells
rung. The where've-you-been-all-day death
that sequesters happiness and finds its home
in desperate friendships, that notifies you of
emergency in the same tepid breath that reveals
a storm is coming soon but shows no proof.
That death where the shopper texts you that
the store is all out of cherry Danishes and I leave
for work while you work from home and you sit
at the kitchen island without me, picking
at the Danish-shaped hole in your heart
like it's a window without a frame.

PREHEATED

Never follow a wormhole to a second location.
Follow your heart to the brick wall that blames
a you-shaped hole. Inside is the love of a good dog,
the love of a good woman, the sound of the oven
just preheated. I put my palm out to a cold nose.
I put myself out there and I'm frowned up and down,
like someone forgot to set a timer on my welcome.
I wish there were another way to say
that I like long walks around the park, with or without
a woman, with or without a dog, whether or not
dinner is waiting for me when I get home.
I wish there were a less cliché way to say
that everything gold must go. But I've been
to the future and back and you wouldn't believe
the things that people there call out of style.
Things that seem so young and fresh today

OBEDIENCE

For the same reason you don't give stray dogs
new names, I don't make eye contact with strangers
in the wild. It's a window to a soul I didn't ask
to access. Humanitarians will tell you to look
for the good in everybody, that it's there, blinking
beneath the rubble of all that consciousness.
They say it like it's easy, like it's a cloudy day
that can be cleared with the push of a broom.
But once the dog starts sticking its paw out
for new acquaintances, it's easy to forget
how many hands it used to bite, before it started
to value the rewards for silence and sitting still.

MOTHER EARTH

The teacher draws the woman and says
that drawing a woman is like drawing a flower,
each curve vining up toward the sun with a purpose,
each inch dependent on the body's connection
to the earth. The teacher draws the man and says
that drawing a man is like drawing a mountain,
peaks jutting up and bolting dramatically, valleys
sweeping flat only to feed the weeds that grow
in the now-dead river of its former self.
While beautiful, every flower we've ever seen
lived briefly and most of the mountains we've seen
were no bigger than a laptop screen. The teacher says
that mountains were made for flattening and flowers
were born to be plucked from the ground.
The teacher keeps pictures of budding mountains
on her desk and her walls are dotted with flowers
that slept only long enough to bloom once.
When we ask what the flower does, the teacher says
they were nourished to sit pretty and when we ask
what the mountain does, she grabs a broom and
dusts the high cliffside clean, to reveal the faces
of all our fathers carved permanently
into the raw materials of Mother Earth.

INVISIBLE

I take pictures of the people
I'll outlive, so one day
I can swipe through them
and remember the days.
This isn't something I started doing
intentionally. I've just always
appreciated candidness over pose.
And one day these people
just started to disappear.
I suppose there's really no way
I can be certain I'll outlive them,
but I can also never be certain
I'll ever see them alive again.
They could be snapping pictures
of me picking my nose, raising
one eyebrow as I fart, pinching up
a peanut well after the five-second
rule has elapsed. And in fact, I hope
they are. I've always wondered
if I'm actually see-through
when I'm at my most invisible.

SMALL TALK SYMPHONY

I want to snap the tail off you and watch it grow
back over time. I want to watch your scales renew
and crunch the old ones beneath my feet
like half a million lifeless leaves. The whole world
bends with sympathy when a loved one dies,
but when you tell them each new day is a loved one
slipping away, their hearts unwind in precious moments
spent like dust in an hourglass of anytimes.
They've had enough and I'm just getting started.
There's no deep endless well of sympathy
for the deep endless flow of need. All bundled up
into a decade and running out of time, a new year
is clawing its first hashmarks in my throat. I woke up
undone like this one morning and never fully fused
back into one real thing.

THIS OLD HOUSE

What if the world's first carpenter
was only trying to fashion the human body
into a vessel we could sleep inside?
A kitchen for a heart, a washroom for a
soul, grandma's collection of knit Afghans
for a head of hair, two little windows
above the fireplace for eyes, one long
broad chimney to waft the outside in?
What if we call the frame the bones
because the world's first carpenter
broke the world's worst bone and saw
the shards poke through the drywall?
Did they think inside we were made of
trees? That the limbs the birds perched on
were god's sick idea of a stick in the mud?
What if they designed the welcome mat
to replicate the human tongue, to speak
in the implication of open doors and ignore
the dirt caught in the tread? What if
my internal organs are only dinner plates
stacked just so, juice glasses placed
upside down to dry, waiting for visitors
to trespass my mind? What if my mind
was designed for carpentry and not to pry
the nails from every seam of this old house?

IDENTICALLY ALIVE

Every day is spent recuperating from one thing
or another. Six months lapse picking at scabs
and friends start pleading *that scar must be at least*
half numb by now, but while the shallow end of my lung
has found a deeper breath, my autumn headaches
have flared up again and election season is fast approaching.
My stubbed toe healed more or less crooked but
on my way home from the dentist I walked by a patron
who'd just exited a restaurant and was asking a homeless
teenager what he'd done to secure employment today,
while he pinched three-dollar bills in front of his face and
wouldn't let go. Some Decembers the winter solstice falls
on my birthday and some it's the day before,
and some seasons it feels like it takes entire years for my body
and mind to prepare for another summer. They call it
regeneration when the earth's face blooms new leaves, but
after watching the old ones fall to the ground
for weeks at a time, year after year, it starts to look
a hell of a lot more like healing, when new flowers
take over the plots of dirt that claimed old flowers
that looked as identically alive as they do now dead.

GRAVE-DIRT NEAR ME

We still discard our garbage
the same ways we always have:
buried deep or burnt far-gone.
These are also the ways we discard
ourselves: either six feet down or ground
to ash. But there's been a plan in the works
for years: to capsule our waste into rockets
and shoot it all off into space,
so it can exit our solar system and orbit
something else.
And one day we might
call home a graveyard
circling another planet's moon
that we could never afford the tickets to.

Joshua Lillie is a sober, bipolar poet from Tucson, Arizona. He and his wife, Clare, have a small home tucked half a mile into the desert. Settled into the solitude there, he's had poems published by numerous journals, zines and presses. He works as a bartender on Historic 4th Avenue in downtown Tucson.